BEATRIC

Somewhere in the Night

BELIEVE + YOU'LL ACHIEVE

KENATE

Somewhere
in the night

Renate Thomas

GRANVILLE ISLAND
PUBLISHING
www.granvilleislandpublishing.com

Library and Archives Canada Cataloguing in Publication

Thomas, Renate, 1953–, author
     Somewhere in the night / Renate Thomas.

Poems.
ISBN 978-1-926991-31-3 (pbk.)

     I. Title.

PS8639.H5888S64 2013   C811'.6   C2013-905300-X

Editor: Michael Kenyon
Cover and text designer: Omar Gallegos
Photographs from the collection of Renate Thomas

Granville Island Publishing Ltd.
212 – 1656 Duranleau St.
Vancouver, BC, Canada V6H 3S4

604-688-0320 / 1-877-688-0320
info@granvilleislandpublishing.com
www.granvilleislandpublishing.com

First published in January 2014
Printed in Canada on recycled paper

I would like to dedicate this book to my friend, Esther Tremblay, who believed in me and encouraged me to reach for the stars. . .

Thanks

Acknowledgements

I wish to thank my lovely daughter Niki for keeping me grounded; her support meant a lot to me.

A special thank you to the team at Granville Island Publishing, especially Jo Blackmore for her assistance. Without her, this book would not have happened.

Contents

Lifeboat Drill

Daisy

Fields of daisies, now all gone
                    Picked and broken
         They lie
Strewn along the sidewalk

Oh daisy, daisy, please tell me
Who my true love some day will be
He loves me, he loves me not. . .
Look up at me through your
Evil yellow eye
Don't act so sly
Whisper softly in my ear
The words of love I want to hear
White petal, the last one left me
Tells me softly that he loves me

I Need Somebody

Is there anybody out there
   Who has some time to share?
Is there anybody who is willing
   To show me that they care?

Is there anybody out there
   Who'll take away my pain?
Is there anybody who is willing
   To make me laugh again?

Is there anybody out there
   Who'll hold me when I cry?
Is there anybody who is willing
   To hug my fears goodbye?

Is there anybody out there?
I need someone to hold me
Is there anybody who is willing?
   I need someone to care

I need someone who will take the time
   I need somebody there
I need someone to love me
   I need someone to love

Moonbeams

Moonbeams of misty dream flakes
    Shadows of things not right
Whispers of howling delusions
    Tears in an empty bed at night

Where is the love we used to share
    The arms that held me tight
Now there's just tears and loneliness
    Where our love once made things right

Dreams and schemes and fairy tales
    Do we dare try again
Or are we just circle-bound
    On a ferris wheel of pain?

Lifetime

A lifetime is a long time, yet
   A long time is a lifetime
If there is no one to share a
   Lifetime with, then
There is no long time, nor a
   Lifetime
There is only yesterday
   Today and tomorrow
And when they are
   Gone
There is nothing
   No one
And you'll yearn
   For your lifetime
But it's a long time
Gone

The Condemned

We are the living dead
Summoned from the deep dark sea
And like zombies we are entranced to follow the
Razor-thin scent of our long
Crusade homeward

For days and days we pilot the
Salty waters
Driven by madness as the scent becomes clearer
Sharper
At the edge of the sea we
Divide
For each has his own creek or
Mountain stream to follow

In quiet waters we rest
For we are weary

Up shallow creeks we swim
The gravel biting
The sun drying our backs
Against rocks we are dashed
Our bellies scraped
Yet we fight to go on
With bleeding, bruised flesh
Charge the rapids, flinging ourselves
Against the crags, a mad rush at the
Blockade of our homeland

Our numbers have diminished
Only the strong and alert have survived
We are weary and worn
Bleeding, bruised, and torn
But we continue for we know that home is just
Beyond that little hill

In peaceful waters
We run the gauntlets
Predators line the waterside
Stalking
Waiting for our leprous forms
Circling in for the kill

We are lifted from the water by
Claws or teeth
We are beaten by clubs
Cast on the water's edge
Our guts squeezed out by a
Boot's pressure
Smiling faces abort us
Leave us gaping on the banks
With rotting bodies

We stall for time
We finished our duty, we are home
We are the living dead
Condemned before we are born

Peace

Blood red roses, all bloomed black
Weeds crawling round a deserted shack
Broken windows, moss-covered tiles
Spooky ghosts with eerie smiles
Gardens ragged, fields burned down
Muddy sidewalks, watered brown
Tiny crosses, worn away
Behind weary trees, where skeletons lay
Bombshells and mangled trees
Rotten canvas blowing in the breeze
A little doll, a shirt, a hat
An arm, a gun, a hungry rat
Deserted grounds, all burned black
Deserted hell, who'll come back?
Where have they gone? A pause, a sigh
Where are we going, you and I?

Sometime

Somewhere my love
We'll meet again
Maybe not today
     Nor tomorrow
But sometime
Not as strangers
     But as lovers
Who have shared an
Eternity
Together
     Tears there shall be none
     Nor memories
     Of all our yesterdays shared
Only tomorrow
And all our tomorrows
To come

Truth

I was on my way to
Where,
When I realized I was
Nowhere
I mingled in a crowd of
Nameless faces
And was
No one
I asked, "Why?"
But got no answer
I said something
But no one listened
I had a friend
He was a back-stabber
I tried to be helpful
But got shot down
I tried to live
Destroying nothing
Asking nothing
Wanting nothing
Destroying nothing
From society
But they scorned me

When I took my life
They asked themselves, "Why?"

Suicide

It was a hot, smouldering day
On the beach a young girl lay
Eyes closed, deep in thought
Heedless to the sound of insects as they fought

Tears stained her slender nose
Her body lay in a strained pose
Her mind was a jungle, tangled and torn
She possessed the look of a child forlorn

No longer could she live a lie
So she passed judgment that she should die
She defied the rightfulness of her birth
Slowly and silently the waters replaced her earth

Seaward Bound

The winds blow cold and lonely
The waves kiss the shore
Seven years you've sailed the sea
You'll sail for several more

The sea captured and claimed you
It claimed you for its own
Now all I have are memories
And a child you've never known

We were so young and foolish
We thought our love was true
But the sea was your only love
Your aim, the sky of blue

But darling please remember
Wherever you will roam
The sea runs forever. . .
But you'll always have a home
In my heart

Brainstorm

When love slowly fades away
Leaving a vacuum of despair
And each day's pressure knocks you down
And no one seems to care

When every day just crawls along
Over the same problems and woes
When nagging tongues and pointing thumbs
Turn friends into deadly foes

When tempers are low and pressures rise
And nothing seems to fit
When ears are blind and eyes are deaf
And you've lost your friendly wit

When the walls are slowly closing in
And you've just got to get away
Then relax my friend; it's not the end
For tomorrow's a brand new day

Silent

Sitting at the water's edge
Drifting in silence
Wrapped up in speechless thoughts
Hypnotizable concentration
        Silent the dark
        Silent the man
        Silent the thoughts

Kids with Balloons

Canada

From the shores of the mighty Pacific
Across the rugged land
To the shores of the Atlantic
As Canada we stand

"United we stand, divided we fall"
Is a slogan we hold high
For as brothers we will stand together
And as brothers we will die

Our forests are green and thriving
Our lakes are clear and blue
Our cities are expanding
There is a little smog too

Yes, Canada is growing
A little every day
And if we stand together
We'll go a long, long way

The PEOPLE make the country
That's what I've heard say
I'm proud to be a Canadian
Hip Hip Hip Hurray!!!!!

Fences

Don't fence me in
Let me wander all around
To learn how to live
To share and to give
Don't fence in my mind
For it needs to widen and grow
Let my soul be alive
Not retarded or slow
Don't fence ME in
For like a wild flower
I will wilt and die
Let me live to be me
Not living a lie
Don't fence me in
With cities overflowing with hate
Let me learn to love my brother
Before it is too late
Stop crowding my soul
For I long to be left alone
Without fences or obstructions
I shall live in my home

Fences may confine my body
But NEVER my MIND

Freckles

Like dandelions that spot a lawn
They're drawn out by the summer sun;
A winter skin, so creamy white
Soon is a freckled one

They come in all shapes and sizes
They vary in contrast and hue;
They make some people happy
And make others blue

Like stardust they are sprinkled on
Like angels' kisses they cling;
Freckles are a sign of new life
Like the robin who comes for spring

I Saw

I saw a rose
>   In open bloom
I saw it cut
>   Into a vase of doom
I saw a bird
>   And watched it fly
I heard a shot
>   As it fell to die
I saw a tree
>   So proud and tall
I heard a saw
>   And watched it fall
I saw a lake
>   That once was green
I saw a sign
>   Keep Out – Unclean
I saw hatred
>   And felt the strain
To forgive and forget
>   And love again
I saw life
>   What's it all for
When there is nothing left
>   And dreams are no more

Alone

When I sit
    I sit alone
When I walk
    I walk alone
When I stand
    I stand alone
When I laugh
    I laugh alone
When I cry
    I cry alone
But when I have money
    It's funny
How many "friends" I have

Life is Like a River

Life is like a river
       Flowing here and there
Stopping sometimes in little pools
       Reflecting, to go on to where

On it's lifelong journey
       It always finds a way
To hurdle over obstacles
       Nature sets in its way

Summertime it's in a hurry
       Sometimes calm and clear
Sometimes eddies and whitecaps
       Sometimes like a mirror

The river of life keeps flowing
       Rushing to meet each day
Never knowing what lies ahead
       Just flowing day by day

Silver Threads

Silver threads of misty magic
Spools of empty dreams
Thimbles of disillusions
Intertwining rays of coloured loneliness
Find the needle's eye
Where does the camel belong?
Weave a wavering thread of existence
Search for the end of the line
Tie it in a knot
And start from there
Leaving a small part of yourself
Behind
In every stitch

Snowflakes

We whirl and we twirl
     In lacy gowns of white
We dance and we prance
     To all hours of the night

We are witty and pretty
     We make the most of our sport
We glide and we slide
     For our existence is so short

We skitter and we flitter
     Like ballerinas, we flow
We cry for we must die
     To become part of the snow

Sometimes

Sometimes I'm big
Sometimes I'm small
Sometimes I'm nothing
Nothing at all

Sometimes I'm high
Sometimes I'm low
Sometimes I'm a flower
That the wind doth blow

I am the flower of
Hatred
And lust doth in my petals lie
I am the evil that makes people
High

I am the power of dreams
Beyond
Mortal consumption
I am the reason for peace of
Mind
And my powers are stolen by
Mankind to transfer into a
Mystic
World

I am the power of
Goodness
Which encircles a poor man's
Mind
Only through
Me
And others like me can this man find his
Freedom

So, friends
Come
And let me show you how easy it is to
Ride
Ride the sky
The cloud of
Happiness and feel
Free
To express your trapped emotions
Put all your
Troubles
Behind you and enter the
World
Of beautiful
Meaning
Which I can give you
Come

Sunshine

You are the sunshine of my life
       Part of the air that I breathe
Your friendship means the world to me
       These feelings you can believe

Cupid has his bow and arrows
       Valentine hearts are true
So please be part of my heart
       And let me be part of yours too

Renate Thomas

The Room

There is a room within my mind
      Where there is a peace I cannot find
It has no walls, it has no floor
      It has no windows, it has no door
It has no lock, it has no key
      But it holds
My most precious memories

Running Where

Running fast, running slow
I'm running hard
But I've nowhere to go
Running round, running long
What or whom am I running from
Running to, running fro
My head is running
All thoughts, I don't know
Find me time
For peace of mind
I can't find my head

People

You think you're such a lady
        You stupid, boring snob
Your nose is always in the air
        You act just like a slob

You are always looking down your nose
        Stabbing people in the back
Your lips always razor-thin
        A smile – your face would crack

You think you are the greatest
        But beauty's just skin deep
Your conceit and self-love
        Just make you a creep

Today

I saw you again
Today
And I was
Saddened
Your eyes were
Begging
Me to ask
But I
Just
Walked by

Angel

I felt a presence
And turned to see
The angel of death
Shadowing me
In his eyes
I could see
My heart
My soul
My destiny

Remember

Remember the day
Up in the hay
When you said you would
If I said you could?
Well, now you're a father
And I am a mother
Little Carrie is here
And so is her brother

Wedding Party

Dreams

Call me a dreamer
Oh, I'm in love
      Head over heels
And yet
I don't know him
Not even his name
But that doesn't matter because
He has a name in my
Dreams
And to me, he is everything
Because he loves me too
Call me a dreamer
But some day, when he says
Hi or
      Smiles
            At me
I will understand
            Because
We know each other

Drifting

I can feel myself drifting
Again
You're getting too close
Gently prying
Emotions laid to rest
I am running
Scared
For I can feel your
Warmth
Trying the door
I am fading away
Turning
Closing my eyes
Wrapping my insecurities
Around me
The door is locked
There is no
Key
Go away

Fool

I'm following an endless emotion
Like dark blue thread
Which leads to an empty
Spool
But where I'll stop at
Who knows
Who knows the thoughts of a
Fool

I kissed him
With my eyes closed
Yet my heart was swallowing
The line
He took my love and left me
With disillusion on my mind

Come and see the compassionate fool
Who drowns in self-pity
'Cause she can't have the
One she loves
And no other will do
So she hopes and waits
But alas, is growing old
Alone

Friendship

This morning
       When I awakened
The sun was shining
       I was happy for I had a
  Friend
I was content

This afternoon it turned
              Cloudy
A thousand tangled
     Snakes
Slithered across the sky
It felt spooky
      As though something was
      Shadowing my happiness
I was puzzled

This evening it is quiet
             And dark
Something is lost
Something is wrong
        For
I am alone
In the dark

Something is Wrong

I know that something is
Wrong
Between us
I don't know
What but I can feel it
We're play-acting our
Lives
Like a movie
No one's a star
But one of us is playing
The lead
Our home has become a
House
Our meals
A pleasant restaurant scene
Our conversation
A script
Our actions are
Mechanical
Our true feelings
Camouflaged
The gap is widening
But alas, we've left no
Bridges

I Love You

Your smile melts my frozen heart
  And sets me all aglow
Now you're always on my mind
  Each day my love does grow

But I hear that you're not right for me
  And I'm not right for you
But each day I love you more
  Through shades of misty blue

So, before I make a fool of myself
  I'll pack my things and go
Let the wind wipe away my trace
  And the words, "I love you so"

The Affair

Why does it have to be
Like this
Cringing and crying inside
Each time I see
You
Longing for the
Warmth
We shared in those
Few times
Together
I knew. . .
I guess I always knew
That you didn't love
Me
Yet I closed my eyes
Against that pain
And I loved you
I love you
But to you I was
Just a somebody
Anyone
A convenience
For your pent-up desire
My eyes are open
And yet
I'm still blind
A fool
Just a fool in
Love

I hate you
God knows how much I
Hate you
Yet all the pain and tears
The endless
Profanities
Flung against you
Cannot erase the
Love
I have for you
I don't know what
To do
My tomorrows
Are tears shed on the
Paths of today
I've tried
Oh God, I've tried so
Hard
To forget
But the nights are too
Short
The days are too
Long
The love too
Deep: today I saw you
Again
And I was sad
'Cause I know it's over
But I also know

It will never be
Over
I hate you
I hate you so much
For using my love
Like a flower uses
The soil
Turning a beautiful
Experience
Into a bad dream
A dirty vulgarity
And yet through
All this
I love you
And like a fool
I am clinging to a
Dream
Because I am
Afraid
Oh god I am so
Afraid
To be let down
Again
To be locked in my mind
Afraid to love
To be loved
Afraid to let my
True feelings
Show

Goodbye

The time has come
For me. . . for me to say
Goodbye
And though my voice
May crack
With unsteadiness
And my eyes brim
With the shadows
Of rainy times. . . I will be strong
And walk away proud. . .
Though one little word
A simple gesture
From you would
Crack my plastered exterior
I will not break down
I will not look back
I will not
Oh God help me
Please help me be strong
Oh it hurts
It hurts so much
For I still love you so. . .
Goodbye my love

If Only You Had Loved Me

If you had loved me
You'd never have made me cry
If you loved me
You'd never have told me a lie
If you loved me
You'd always have been true
If you loved me
As much as I loved you

If you loved me
You'd have taken the time to understand
If you loved me
You'd have been there to hold my hand
If you loved me
You'd have shared yourself with me
If you loved me
Totally

If you loved me
You'd never have let me down
If you loved me
You'd have never played around
If you loved me
The way true love should be
If you loved me
You'd have had my love eternally

Oh, If only you had loved me
It could have been so grand
Lovers together, always
        Hand in hand
Nothing would have been
            Too hard to bear
If only you had loved me
Enough to always be there

But you didn't love me
It showed in every way
While my love was growing
        Yours began to stray

Disillusions grew within my heart
Every day was filled with pain
Slowly I locked up my heart
        I'll not open it again

It's too late to say, I'm sorry
            Your words are never true
There's been too many "sorrys"
            And promises untrue

If only you had loved me
Half as much as I loved you
It could have been so wonderful
        But you didn't

If Only. . .

If only you could see
You
Through my eyes
If only you would
Walk a mile in my
Shoes
Maybe you'd think a bit
Before you criticize and
Abuse

I am only me
Myself
Not a carbon copy of
You
I make mistakes
I'm only
Human
Aren't you?

So, take a long look
In your own back
Yard
Search through your
Closets
And maybe you'll find
That people in glass
Houses
Shouldn't throw stones
'Cause
One might find
You!

Long Ago

Long ago, visions of white
    Smiles, best wishes, feelings high
Gifts, a cake and waltzes
    And dreams that touched the sky

Loving days of sharing life
    Sharing dreams like lovers do
We gave each other many things
    God, how much I loved you

The dreams went on dreaming
    But I still believed in you
I followed you down every road
    But I was losing you

It came so slowly that we didn't see
    The signs of things falling apart
We turned our heads so as not to see
    The pain when it did start

The lovers were now two people
    Struggling to achieve
A fairytale of happiness
    That others would believe

The lies, harsh words, the loneliness
    The not knowing how to cope
Not believing a single word
    Giving up the hope

Fights, lawyers, court, legal documents
    Signing a marriage away
Two lovers of long ago
    On a divided highway

Too Many Tears

Too many tears in
    Too many years
Frustration and pain
    Nothing to gain
Sorrys and promises
    Never sincere
Dreams and fantasies
    That never did appear
We said goodbye
    When we did part
You followed your dreams
    I followed my heart
I picked up the pieces
    Reconstructed my life
You pretended you didn't care
    And took a new wife
But I saw through your actions
    Your dreams and your lies
I saw that you still loved me
    It was always there in your eyes
So often I tried to explain
    To make you see
That wishing we were together again
    Was just your fantasy
You were fanning your own ashes
    Mine died long ago

Letting Go

Tonight I lit a candle
    And through its flame
I felt your presence
    I heard you call my name

You wrapped your arms around me
    You wiped away my tear
And softly you whispered
    That you'd always be near

I cried tears of anger
    Frustration and pain
How could you go and leave me
    It'll never be the same

You tried to make me understand
    That life doesn't always play fair
And sometimes we have to leave
    It doesn't mean we don't care

I felt you slowly slip away
    I tried to hold on strong
The candle gently flickered
    Your presence had gone

Tonight I lit a candle
    I lit a whole damn row
I saw your smiling face
    Saying, it's time to let go!

Night

Mr. Self-Conscious and Me

I was alone
Alone
Alone
All alone
In the dark
Creeping corner of
My room
We were alone
Alone
Alone
All alone
When he torpedoed
My image
And left me
Bleeding, defenseless
Thousands of voices
Buzzed through the air
But no one was there

Except for my naked mind
And me
We were alone
Alone, all, all alone
When he stabbed
Me with unseeing eyes
Dragged me through hell's
Fire
Then left
Me alone with a twisted mind
Facedown in
Despair
I was alone
Alone
Alone
All alone

Delusions

I sit here alone in the darkness
    Trying to recapture my childhood dreams
Which have eluded me since
    Somewhere between adolescence and reality

I lost my ability to give and receive love
    When my father died and left me
Without a friend and so alone
    To face a conquering society

I learnt to adopt an attitude
    When I married a man I didn't love
Because he was the monkey on my back
    My own private road to hell

I possessed the power to shrink and retreat
    When my sensitivity would bleed
With the constant insults, emotional violence
    I endured in the name of holy matrimony

I kept my shame and embarrassment
    Burning deep inside me
As I smiled and played the people game
    Of lovers happily ever after

I struggled hard to keep my pride
    Let him take my self-respect
And slash my hopes and murder my dreams
    He would never break my pride

We were on a course straight to hell
  But I stopped long enough to smell the roses
And when the life came back to my eyes
  I left him and never looked back

For seven long years I've struggled
  To achieve a sort of sense to all the ashes
That I'd left behind in the name of marriage
  For better or worse, worser, worsest

I forgave him for all his foolish behavior
  But I'll always live in the memory
That I've lost the ability to be whole
  The girl I used to be

Sometimes I cry alone in the darkness
  Till I'm too tired and feel empty
Yet face the world with a smile
  Because it's my life

So, please don't ask of me
  What I cannot give
I will be a friend forever
  I will always be there when needed

But never ask of me
  What I cannot give

Depression

Depression is me
    I am depression
It's eating my brain
Destroying my emotions
It's killing me
And I haven't got the will to
Fight it
Maybe heaven can wait
But how much longer
Can I wait
For
Heaven?

Enemy

I am my worst
Enemy
I am slowly killing
Myself
I am the judge
The jury
I am the prosecutor
I am the witness
The sentence is
Solitary
Confinement
To myself
I am lost in the
Maze
Of my being
Doomed to the
Twilight zone of my
Mind

Hell's Paradise

Yesterday's fears rip through my brain as I try to catch a
Morsel of common sense. My mind is deteriorating behind these bars
Of hell. Life is a dream; there is no reality behind these bars;
Only yesterday's dreams penetrate. The days are countless; the
Hours are years; time slips by unnoticed. There is no such thing as
Time where I am. Time is a figment. Was there ever such a thing
As time?

The cold fingers of morning squeeze through the cage's window.
A few straggling rays of sunlight dance on the drab walls of Hell's
Paradise. Another day is born, but for me it is unmeaning. Time
And the World are strangers to me.

I've got to get out of here. I can't stand this quietness where
I can hear my breath and the rumble of my guts. I am on the brink of
Insanity, yet those animals feel that my nature is improving; they're
Teaching me a lesson, so they say. Yet what my eyes cannot see my
Mind has learned to draw. And if I were an Angel I'd sprout wings
And fly out of this cage into mercy.

Am I sorry for what I did? Well, maybe I should be, but I've
Been in this God-forsaken place for so long that I've forgotten what
I've done.

The guard comes to the door and orders me to stand back, so he
Can enter safely (as if I were a savage). He throws me looks of hatred
Then says, "Tomorrow you'll be released." But no feeling
Of surprise or happiness tickles my spine. The savage instinct
And pride that once flowed thick in my veins have been crushed and
Erased by the long years of depression. My spirit is broken
Like a stallion's after he has been broken. Was I ever human?
All my spirits are decayed and now they set me free
Into the world that long ago rejected and flung
Me behind bars to weaken my senses. A world that has changed its
Face like a woman changes hers. I am afraid to go back to civilization,
Afraid of its inhabitants, afraid of being inferior. I do not want
To go back to face the proud people. I don't want to be left
Alone again. I am afraid, oh God, I am afraid.

In the Darkness

The sea of desperation
    Is flowing through my mind
In darkness I stumble
    The answers I cannot find
To be a breeze
    And blow away
To places… I do not know
    To leave behind
A tormented mind
    And feelings so low
To run and hide
    To seek to find
The answers of the time
    To reach a star
That is way too far
    These things I do not know
To find a place of silence
    A place to laugh and sing
To be alone, never at home
    This tiring search. . .
When will it be over

Michael

Michael hides behind dark allies
Watching and waiting to ravish the
Young children
Yes, Michael sold by the peddler
The devil of darkness and abuse
With greedy hands gloats over his
Victims as the spider gloats over his spun fly
Hanging dizzy in the tangles, web of life
He'll strip you of everything you own
Then leave you bleeding in the alley
All alone
Crying and cursing his name
For you need him so bad
That your guts are splitting
You grovel on the pavement
For the emptiness is so great
Then you start to run
You must out-run him
And you run and run and run
The faster you run the greater is the pain
You've lost control
And deep, deep down inside
You can feel Michael laughing at you
He just laughs and laughs and laughs
"Oh you bastard, you filthy bastard!"
You scream
Feeling the splinters of obstruction
Something warm is running down your face
And then there is nothing

Moody Blues

I am angry at the world
So let my anger flame
Let it roar until the ashes die
Let it soar to the highest denominator
Then crash to the deepest sea
Like a bird shot in flight

I am angry at myself
For I am entangled in the roots of fury
Trapped by the bonds of emotion
Burning in a sea of desperation
I am lost in hell's fire
Burning till the death of the world

I am angry at my life
For I am ruining myself
Hiding behind the hands of timidity
Wishing to shout out my questions
But instead pausing and yearning deep inside
For the answers to my question, "Why?"

I am angry at my mind
For trying to destroy my faith in me
And I know that I must fight against it
For I must trust myself
My tears of self-pity are in vain
For I am losing faith

Loneliness

Loneliness is
> An unending dark void

Depression is
> No hope

Loneliness is
> An aching emptiness

Depression is
> No dreams

Loneliness is
> Anguished, tangled feelings

Depression is
> No emotions

Loneliness is
> Forced laughter

Depression is
> Dark consuming

Loneliness is
> Tears of frustration

Depression is
> No feelings

Loneliness has
> Friends

Depression has
> Nobody!

Searching

Standing in front of the looking
Glass
Arranging the cobwebs of my
Existence
Looking for something that's
Always been there
But
Hidden in a disguise
I cannot
Conquer
   And the devil shares
My looking glass
Sharing my
Vanity
As his wispy fingers
Paint
Over my
Mask
Transform me into an
Image
Of woman
Leeringly he drapes clothes
Around my naked
Flesh

Beware my eyes, you
Poor
Stupid fool
As they burn into your
Wretched soul
I shall destroy your
Dreams
My love
Like you crushed mine
So long ago
Fantasies will cease
And reality
Shall rear its
Ugly head
And force open your
Star-glazed eyes
Fate shall be your
Friend
But beware of friends
They smile white teeth
Phantom expressions
Baring fangs
Wielding knives
Oh you poor stupid
Carbon copy of
Existence
Why do you lie to
Yourself
Can't you see God is
Dead

Why do you cling
To a
Myth
    Rebel, I say
Scream it loud
And run away
Try to hide
But where is
Freedom
This God we are fighting for
Where does he exist?
How many will die
Bearing his name
In the vanity of a
Pot-bellied general
    Come on people
Snap out of your little shells
Look into your looking
glasses
Face reality
No matter
How long
You try
You'll never gain freedom
For freedom
Is only a
State of
Mind

Uptight

Red light
Orange light
Waiting for the go light!
Eyes bright
Blinker flashing right
Speeding through
A drunken night
Feeling kind of uptight
Just had a knife fight
Now on a ghost flight
Blinker out
Going right
Roaring through
Town on a Friday night
Headlights flashing
Just lost my eyesight
Jammed on the brakes tight
Sighed in a bird's fright
Felt a slashing pain
In my right
I smashed up all right
Out went the life light!

Ten Little Cops

Ten little cops all sitting in a row
A call came in; now which one ought to go?
Old Samuel turned and said to big Charley
"It's time for our break, we're having coffee
And besides it's already half-past eight
My order of eggs will be ruined if I'm late!"
Another cop turned his head to say
"Don't count on us; we worked yesterday
And besides we're tired, for you see
We helped this kitten down from a tree."
Numbers five and six said, "We cannot go
We chased this fellow, our gas is low
And besides we did our duty last night
We were called to stop a husband-wife fight!"
Number four hesitantly turned to number three
Whose eyes were closed; snoring peaceably
"We won't take it, it's not our line
And besides we worked last night till ten to nine!"
Then number one turned to number two
Saying, "Well, I guess it's up to me and you
We're already late so we'll run the stops
After all *we* are duty-bound cops."

Yesterday's World

I dream yesterday's dream
I walk yesterday's street
I do the same things every day
I know it's myself I cheat

I dream of all those booze parties
That really were wild
I think about the tears I shed
Over my still-born child

Oh God, help me, you must help me
Escape this cruel world of mankind
Oh God, take me to the Angel's land
To restore my peace of mind

Renate

I stand here alone, like a
Fool
On the hill
Watching the world
Crawl past my feet

I feel nothing
Just a hacking emptiness
In my robot
Container
Letting the wind's
      — fingers
Rake
Through
My autumn hair

I exist in that
—

That valley of carbon-copied
Mankind

Up here on the
Hill
I'm
An individual
And my mind runs free

My bonds are air-borne
In stolen pieces of
Time
I can be me
Without fear of
Inferiority

I can laugh at my images
Oh my mind
Is such a brilliant
Play-toy
When allowed to cut
Loose to foolishness

Yesterday I had a love
In that
Valley
But he's dead
And gone to
Memories
Of time shared

My sorrow rides the
Winds
My tears are faucets
My heart is dead

I feel so useless
So alone
And
Yet I have friends
But they can't bridge the
Gap
Of time
In my existence
They don't know how I
Feel
When I wear a
Smile
Like a broach

With a lump in my
Throat

Can't you see
I'm like a fly
Dashing in blind
Fury
Hurling myself into the
Spider's web
Hanging there
Suspended
Struggling for survival
Yet wishing a
Swift
Painless
Death

Darkness is reaching out
Greedy talons
Beware the mysteries
It covers

I must descend from my
Throne of
Fantasies
And once again
Enter into the
Mechanical world

Can't you see I am
Silently
Screaming for help
Someone please, lift these
Pressures from my
Mind
I am struggling within
Myself
Only to keep knocking
Myself down deeper
Somebody, please, straighten
Out my wiring
Somebody, please, give me
Security
Life

The winds are chilling my
Face
Where the tears
Lay bare my
Sorrows
It's time to crawl
Home defeated. . .

Where it goes from here & where it will end,
who knows, time may heal the wounds, or
time fade the pain, and yet time may stop,
accidentally, mechanically, or purposely.

Somewhere in the Night

Midnight madness
    Kisses and giggles in the dark
Dreams and promises
    Confidences whispered
Flying high on love
    Sexual fantasies fulfilled
Each a promise
    Of better things to come

The night is gone
    Tears rain
Alone
The dreams are shattered
    Deep emptiness
    Tangled emotions
    Anger directed at your own
Foolishness
For believing
In fairytales
    Of happily ever after

Somewhere in the night
There'll be midnight madness
Kisses and giggles in the dark
Dreams and promises
But alas
There is also the daylight
That erases the stars
    Illusions fade
    Reality reigns

A Slice of Time: Tanner's Ashes

Today
> You and I

Took a heartwarming walk
> On the child side

I held your essence
> In my hands

And with Love
> And a brimming

Heart
> I released you

Into the wind

Around your favourite place

And as the wind

Scattered your being

Some blew in my face

On my being, I smiled

And held memories

Under my fingernails
> As I clung to you

For a little while longer
> I felt so much love as

Your essence seeped into me
> And once again

I felt like a part of you
> Intertwined

Forever
> In the destiny

Called life

Iceberg alert on-board ship Queen Elizabeth II coming to Canada, August 1957; my family on far left, my brother Dieter, and me in front of my mother Elfriede.

Birthday celebration on board; me holding balloon at left, Dieter in front.

On ship, me dining with my father Heinrich and Dieter. Mother was sea sick.

Getting ready to attend my stepson Jim Thomas's graduation in Terrace, June 1987.

With Jim, his girlfriend and her mother on his graduation day.

Tanner on his dad Ron's bike, summer 1994.

Tanner on his own Harley Davidson, Christmas 1994.

Tanner wearing his favorite biker outfit, spring 1995.

Tanner and his baby sister in pram, summer 1995.

Tanner welcoming his little sister Niki.

Niki and Tanner cooling off in the back yard, Kitimat 1997.

Tanner on a ride, Kitimat 1998.

A salute from a dirty Tanner, Cultus Lake 1998.

Niki all dressed up, 1998.

Niki and Tanner ready to watch a
home-movie, 1998

Tanner playing with his robots, 1999.

Tanner graduating from preschool, 1998

Niki and Tanner enjoying snow cones, Chilliwack fair, August 1999.

Renate Thomas was born in 1953 in Germany and immigrated to Canada in 1957, where she has resided ever since. She became a Canadian citizen in 2005. Thomas has worked at tree-planting, various jobs in the lumber industry, such as manufacturing picket-fence posts and telephone poles, and on the green chain. She also drove an eighty-ton truck for a mining company.

In the midst of that busy life, she married and had two children. But the marriage did not last, and a car accident later robbed her of her eldest child. Renate picked up the pieces of her life, had a stint picking fiddlehead greens in the forests around Prince George, and later moved to Calgary. She eventually moved back to Terrace, BC and worked for the school board for ten years. Thomas now resides in the Fraser Valley city of Chilliwack, BC, the town in which she grew up.

"Life as I knew it," she said, "ended on August 16, 1999, with the loss of my son and my personal injury." Expressing her deepest emotions in her poetry helped Thomas recover, collect herself and put things in perspective.